SYNTHESISER MODULES

Table of Contents

Analog sequencer 1
Band-pass filter 2
Band-stop filter 3
Digital filter 4
High-pass filter 7
Low-frequency oscillation 9
Low-pass filter 10
Music sequencer 13
Variable-gain amplifier 20
Voltage-controlled filter 21
Voltage-controlled oscillator 21

Preface

Each chapter in this book ends with a URL to a hyperlinked online version. Use the online version to access related pages, websites, footnotes, tables, color photos, updates, or to see the chapter's contributors. Click the edit link to suggest changes. Please type the URL exactly as it appears. If you change the URL's capitalization, for example, it may not work.

Purchase of this book entitles you to a free trial membership in the publisher's book club at www.booksllc.net. (Time limited offer.) Simply enter the barcode number from the back cover onto the membership form on our home page. The book club entitles you to select from millions of books at no additional charge, including a PDF copy of this and related books to read on the go. Simply enter the title or subject onto the search form to find them.

If you have any questions, could you please be so kind as to consult our Frequently Asked Questions page at www.booksllc.net/faqs.cfm? You are also welcome to contact us there.

Publisher: Books LLC, Wiki Series, Memphis, TN, USA, 2013.

Analog sequencer

Typical analog sequencer (Korg SQ-10)

Moog 960 Sequential Controller module (right mid) on Moog Modular 55

An **analog sequencer** is a music sequencer constructed from analogue electronics. The analog sequencer was invented in the first half of the 20th century.

Raymond Scott designed and constructed some of the first electro-mechanical music sequencers during the 1940s. In 1951, computer music including music sequence, music composition and sound generation were started, however, RCA Mark II Sound Synthesizer in 1957 was still indirectly controlled via punch-tape system similar to piano rolls. Also in earlier electronic music, sound-on-film technology was used not only for generating sound waves but also for controlling sequence of note. In addition, cylinder with pins typically used on music box has at least several hundreds years of history on music sequences. Their peculiarities and limitations left a lasting stylistic imprint on Berlin School electronic music, and hence, indirectly, in many later rhythmic synthesizer-driven music genres such as techno, trance music, 1980s synth pop, house, ...

At its most basic, an analog sequencer is nothing but a bank of potentiometers and a "clock" that steps through these potentiometers one at a time and then cycles back to the beginning. The output of the sequencer is fed (as a control voltage and gate pulse) to a synthesizer. By "tuning" the potentiometers, a short repetitive rhythmic motif or riff can be set up.

The most commonly used analog sequencer was the Moog 960, which was a module of the Moog modular synthesizer. It basically consisted of three parallel banks of eight potentiometers: the three banks could either steer three different VCOs to allow three-note chords in the sequence, or (for example) one row could steer pitch while the second row is patched through to the filter cutoff or VCA volume, and a third steers filter cutoff for a white noise generator (thus creating an extremely primitive electronic drum track).

Under each of the eight steps, a switch offered three options: play this step, skip this step, or loop back to the beginning. In order to avoid the monotony of endlessly repeated sequences, pioneering e-musicians like Chris Franke of Tangerine Dream and Michael Hoenig would manipulate these switches in real time during performance, adding and dropping notes and beats from a sequence. Also, the "pitch" row can be patched to two or more oscillators tuned to intervals, and the oscillators mixed in and out one at a time.

Good examples of all these techniques can be heard on the Phaedra, Rubycon, Ricochet, and Encore albums of Tangerine Dream, as well as on Departure from the Northern Wasteland by Michael Hoenig.

By synchronizing two sequencers,

and manipulating them individually, swirling polyrhythmic phasing patterns (as introduced in minimalist music by Steve Reich) can be set up. The title track of the abovementioned Michael Hoenig album is an excellent example.

An additional module (Moog 962) allowed "daisy-chaining" the three rows to form one longer 24-step sequence. In addition, a switch on the 960 itself allowed the third (bottom) row to be used for note lengths.

The output voltage of the sequencer can be added to the output voltage of a keyboard controller, and the latter used to transpose the sequence on the fly. Klaus Schulze was particularly fond of this technique, which lays the musical foundation for tracks like "Bayreuth Return" from Timewind, "Floating" from Moondawn, and indeed pretty much any rhythmic piece from Klaus Schulze's "analog" years. Vangelis and Jean-Michel Jarre likewise availed themselves of this technique.

Except in a temperature-controlled environment after warmup, pitch stability could be problematic. On the famous opening of Phaedra, the sequencer had drifted out of tune, and one can clearly hear Chris Franke retuning the sequence by ear in real time.

Analog sequencers, have in some respects, been replaced by digital devices and software implementations. However, there is a continued interest by modular analog synthesists, who appreciate the real time control offered by the analog sequencer as evidenced by the 'Oberkorn' machine by Analog Solutions, amongst others.

Various analog sequencers

One of the 1st commercially available analog sequencer (front, 3×8 step and 3×16 step) on Buchla 100 (1964/1966)

Earlier Moog sequencer (left, possibly later added) on the 1st *commercially sold* Moog Modular prototype (c.1964)

ARP 1027 Clocked Sequential Control Module (3rd~4th right, 3×10 step) on ARP 2500 (1970)

EML Sequencer 400 (top ×2, 6×16 step) on EML ElectroComp modular synthesizer (1970)

Analog sequencer (right) at Studio BEA 5, Institute of Sonology.

Buchla *250e* Arbitrary Function Generator

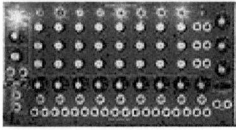

A *Moog 960* clone, Synthesizers.com *Q960* Sequential Controller

Roland System 100M Model 182 Sequencer
Source http://en.wikipedia.org/wiki/Analog_sequencer

Band-pass filter

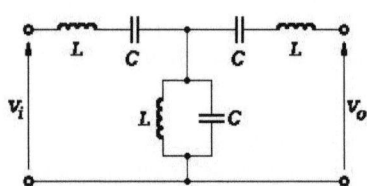

A medium-complexity example of a band-pass filter.

A **band-pass filter** is a device that passes frequencies within a certain range and rejects (attenuates) frequencies outside that range.

Optical band-pass filters are of common usage.

An example of an analogue electronic band-pass filter is an RLC circuit (a resistor–inductor–capacitor circuit). These filters can also be created by combining a low-pass filter with a high-pass filter.

Bandpass is an adjective that describes a type of filter or filtering process; it is to be distinguished from passband, which refers to the actual portion of affected spectrum. Hence, one might say "A dual bandpass filter has two passbands." A *bandpass signal* is a signal containing a band of frequencies away from zero frequency, such as a signal that comes out of a bandpass filter.

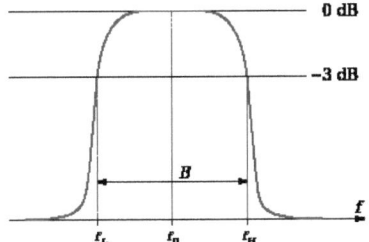

Bandwidth measured at half-power points (gain -3 dB, √2/2, or about 0.707 relative to peak) on a diagram showing magnitude transfer function versus frequency for a band-pass filter.

An ideal bandpass filter would have a completely flat passband (e.g. with no gain/attenuation throughout) and would completely attenuate all frequencies outside the passband. Additionally, the transition out of the passband would be instantaneous in frequency. In practice, no bandpass filter is ideal. The filter does not attenuate all frequencies outside the desired frequency range completely; in particular, there is a region just outside the intended passband where frequencies are attenuated, but not rejected. This is known as the filter roll-off, and it is usually expressed in dB of attenuation per octave or decade of frequency. Generally, the design of a filter seeks to make the roll-off as narrow as possible, thus allowing the filter to perform as close as possible to its intended design. Often, this is achieved at the expense of pass-band or stop-band *ripple*.

The bandwidth of the filter is simply the difference between the upper and lower cutoff frequencies. The shape factor is the ratio of bandwidths measured using two different attenuation values to determine the cutoff frequency, e.g., a shape factor of 2:1 at 30/3 dB means the bandwidth measured between frequencies at 30 dB attenuation is twice that measured between frequencies at 3 dB attenuation.

Outside of electronics and signal processing, one example of the use of band-pass filters is in the atmospheric sciences. It is common to band-pass filter recent meteorological data with a period range of, for example, 3 to 10 days, so that only cyclones remain as fluctuations in the data fields.

In neuroscience, visual cortical simple cells were first shown by David Hubel and Torsten Wiesel to have response properties that resemble Gabor filters, which are band-pass.

Q-factor

A band-pass filter can be characterised by its Q-factor. The Q-factor is the inverse of the fractional bandwidth. A high-Q filter will have a narrow passband and a low-Q filter will have a wide passband. These are respectively referred to as narrow-band and wide-band filters.

In popular culture

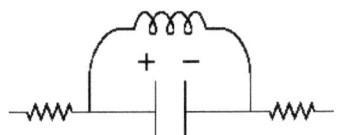

The schematic showing "Kilroy", which Pynchon said represents part of a band-pass filter. His drawing actually resembles the schematic of a band-stop filter.

In his first novel, *V.*, Thomas Pynchon quips that the popular graffiti character Kilroy "had sprung into life, in truth, as part of a band-pass filter".
Source http://en.wikipedia.org/wiki/Band-pass_filter

Band-stop filter

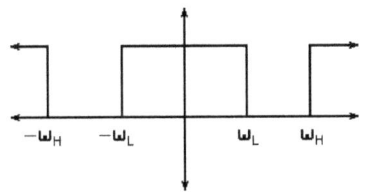

A generic ideal band-stop filter, showing both positive and negative angular frequencies

In signal processing, a **band-stop filter** or **band-rejection filter** is a filter that passes most frequencies unaltered, but attenuates those in a specific range to very low levels. It is the opposite of a band-pass filter. A **notch filter** is a band-stop filter with a narrow stopband (high Q factor).

Narrow notch filters (optical) are used in Raman spectroscopy, live sound reproduction (public address systems, or PA systems) and in instrument amplifiers (especially amplifiers or preamplifiers for acoustic instruments such as acoustic guitar, mandolin, bass instrument amplifier, etc.) to reduce or prevent audio feedback, while having little noticeable effect on the rest of the frequency spectrum (electronic or software filters). Other names include 'band limit filter', 'T-notch filter', 'band-elimination filter', and 'band-reject filter'.

Typically, the width of the stopband is 1 to 2 decades (that is, the highest frequency attenuated is 10 to 100 times the lowest frequency attenuated). However, in the audio band, a notch filter has high and low frequencies that may be only semitones apart.

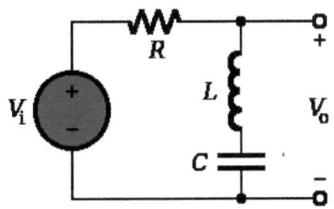

Generic electrical schematic of a simple band-stop filter

Examples

In the audio domain
Anti-hum filter
For countries using 60 Hz power lines:
Low Freq: 59 Hz

High Freq: 61 Hz
This means that the filter passes all frequencies, except for the range of 59–61 Hz. This would be used to filter out the mains hum from the 60 Hz power line, though its higher harmonics could still be present.

For countries where power transmission is at 50Hz, the filter would have a 49–51 Hz range.

Anti-presence filter
Low Freq: 1 kHz
High Freq: 4 kHz
For attenuating presence.

In the radio frequency (RF) domain
Non-linearities of power amplifiers
When measuring the non-linearities of power amplifiers, a very narrow notch filter can be very useful to avoid the carrier frequency. Use of the filter may ensure that the maximum input power of a spectrum analyser used to detect spurious content will not be exceeded.

Wave trap
A notch filter, usually a simple LC circuit, is used to remove a specific interfering frequency. This is a technique used with radio receivers that are so close to a transmitter that it swamps all other signals. The wave trap is used to remove, or greatly reduce, the signal from the local transmitter.

In the optical domain
Optical notch filters rely on destructive interference.
Source http://en.wikipedia.org/wiki/Band-stop_filter

Digital filter

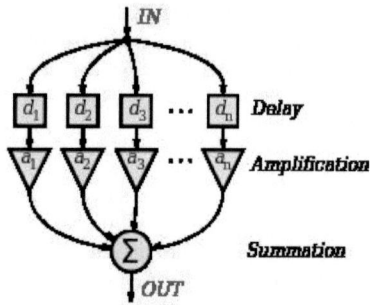

A general finite impulse response filter with n stages, each with an independent delay, d, and amplification gain, a.

In electronics, computer science and mathematics, a **digital filter** is a system that performs mathematical operations on a sampled, discrete-time signal to reduce or enhance certain aspects of that signal. This is in contrast to the other major type of electronic filter, the analog filter, which is an electronic circuit operating on continuous-time analog signals. An analog signal may be processed by a digital filter by first being digitized and represented as a sequence of numbers, then manipulated mathematically, and then reconstructed as a new analog signal (see digital signal processing). In an analog filter, the input signal is "directly" manipulated by the circuit.

A digital filter system usually consists of an analog-to-digital converter to sample the input signal, followed by a microprocessor and some peripheral components such as memory to store data and filter coefficients etc. Finally a digital-to-analog converter to complete the output stage. Program Instructions (software) running on the microprocessor implement the digital filter by performing the necessary mathematical operations on the numbers received from the ADC. In some high performance applications, an FPGA or ASIC is used instead of a general purpose microprocessor, or a specialized DSP with specific paralleled architecture for expediting operations such as filtering.

Digital filters may be more expensive than an equivalent analog filter due to their increased complexity, but they make practical many designs that are impractical or impossible as analog filters. Since digital filters use a sampling process and discrete-time processing, they experience latency (the difference in time between the input and the response), which is almost irrelevant in analog filters.

Digital filters are commonplace and an essential element of everyday electronics such as radios, cellphones, and stereo receivers.

Characterization of digital filters
A digital filter is characterized by its transfer function, or equivalently, its difference equation. Mathematical analysis of the transfer function can describe how it will respond to any input. As such, designing a filter consists of developing specifications appropriate to the problem (for example, a second-order low pass filter with a specific cut-off frequency), and then producing a transfer function which meets the specifications.

The transfer function for a linear, time-invariant, digital filter can be expressed as a transfer function in the Z-domain; if it is causal, then it has the form:

$$H(z) = \frac{B(z)}{A(z)} = \frac{b_0 + b_1 z^{-1} + b_2 z^{-2} + \cdots + b_N z^{-N}}{1 + a_1 z^{-1} + a_2 z^{-2} + \cdots + a_M z^{-M}}$$

where the order of the filter is the greater of N or M. See Z-transform's LCCD equation for further discussion of this transfer function.

This is the form for a recursive filter with both the inputs (Numerator) and outputs (Denominator), which typically leads to an IIR infinite impulse response behaviour, but if the denominator is made equal to unity i.e. no feedback, then this becomes an FIR or finite impulse response filter.

Analysis techniques
A variety of mathematical techniques may be employed to analyze the behaviour of a given digital filter. Many of these analysis techniques may also be employed in designs, and often form the basis of a filter specification.

Typically, one analyzes filters by calculating how the filter will respond to a simple input such as an impulse response. One can then extend this information to visualize the filter's response to more complex signals. Riemann spheres have been used, together with

Impulse response

The impulse response, often denoted $h[k]$ or h_k, is a measurement of how a filter will respond to the Kronecker delta function. For example, given a difference equation, one would set $x_0 = 1$ and $x_k = 0$ for $k \neq 0$ and evaluate. The impulse response is a characterization of the filter's behaviour. Digital filters are typically considered in two categories: infinite impulse response (IIR) and finite impulse response (FIR). In the case of linear time-invariant FIR filters, the impulse response is exactly equal to the sequence of filter coefficients:

$$y_n = \sum_{k=0}^{n-1} h_k x_{n-k}$$

IIR filters on the other hand are recursive, with the output depending on both current and previous inputs as well as previous outputs. The general form of an IIR filter is thus:

$$\sum_{m=0}^{M-1} a_m y_{n-m} = \sum_{k=0}^{n-1} b_k x_{n-k}$$

Plotting the impulse response will reveal how a filter will respond to a sudden, momentary disturbance.

Difference equation

In discrete-time systems, the digital filter is often implemented by converting the transfer function to a linear constant-coefficient difference equation (LCCD) via the Z-transform. The discrete frequency-domain transfer function is written as the ratio of two polynomials. For example:

$$H(z) = \frac{(z+1)^2}{(z-\frac{1}{2})(z+\frac{3}{4})}$$

This is expanded:

$$H(z) = \frac{z^2 + 2z + 1}{z^2 + \frac{1}{4}z - \frac{3}{8}}$$

and divided by the highest order of z:

$$H(z) = \frac{1 + 2z^{-1} + z^{-2}}{1 + \frac{1}{4}z^{-1} - \frac{3}{8}z^{-2}} = \frac{Y(z)}{X(z)}$$

The coefficients of the denominator, a_k, are the 'feed-backward' coefficients and the coefficients of the numerator are the 'feed-forward' coefficients, b_k. The resultant linear difference equation is:

$$y[n] = -\sum_{k=1}^{N} a_k y[n-k] + \sum_{k=0}^{M} b_k x[n-k]$$

or, for the example above:

$$\frac{Y(z)}{X(z)} = \frac{1 + 2z^{-1} + z^{-2}}{1 + \frac{1}{4}z^{-1} - \frac{3}{8}z^{-2}}$$

rearranging terms:

$$\Rightarrow (1 + \tfrac{1}{4}z^{-1} - \tfrac{3}{8}z^{-2})Y(z) = (1 + 2z^{-1} + z^{-2})X(z)$$

then by taking the inverse z-transform:

$$\Rightarrow y[n] + \tfrac{1}{4}y[n-1] - \tfrac{3}{8}y[n-2] = x[n] + 2x[n-1] + x[n-2]$$

and finally, by solving for $y[n]$:

$$y[n] = -\tfrac{1}{4}y[n-1] + \tfrac{3}{8}y[n-2] + x[n] + 2x[n-1] + x[n-2]$$

This equation shows how to compute the next output sample, $y[n]$, in terms of the past outputs, $y[n-p]$, the present input, $x[n]$, and the past inputs, $x[n-p]$. Applying the filter to an input in this form is equivalent to a Direct Form I or II realization, depending on the exact order of evaluation.

Filter design

The design of digital filters is a deceptively complex topic. Although filters are easily understood and calculated, the practical challenges of their design and implementation are significant and are the subject of much advanced research.

There are two categories of digital filter: the recursive filter and the nonrecursive filter. These are often referred to as infinite impulse response (IIR) filters and finite impulse response (FIR) filters, respectively.

Filter realization

After a filter is designed, it must be *realized* by developing a signal flow diagram that describes the filter in terms of operations on sample sequences.

A given transfer function may be realized in many ways. Consider how a simple expression such as $ax + bx + c$ could be evaluated – one could also compute the equivalent $x(a+b) + c$. In the same way, all realizations may be seen as "factorizations" of the same transfer function, but different realizations will have different numerical properties. Specifically, some realizations are more efficient in terms of the number of operations or storage elements required for their implementation, and others provide advantages such as improved numerical stability and reduced round-off error. Some structures are better for fixed-point arithmetic and others may be better for floating-point arithmetic.

Direct Form I

A straightforward approach for IIR filter realization is Direct Form I, where the difference equation is evaluated directly. This form is practical for small filters, but may be inefficient and impractical (numerically unstable) for complex designs. In general, this form requires 2N delay elements (for both input and output signals) for a filter of order N.

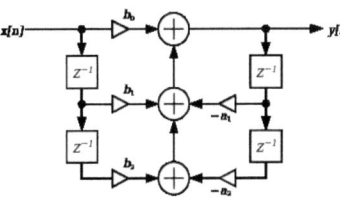

Direct Form II

The alternate Direct Form II only needs N delay units, where N is the order of the filter – potentially half as much as Direct Form I. This structure is obtained by reversing the order of the numerator and denominator sections of Direct Form I, since they are in fact two linear systems, and the commutativity property applies. Then, one will notice that there are two columns of delays (z^{-1}) that tap off the center net, and these can be combined since they are redundant, yielding the implementation as shown below.

The disadvantage is that Direct Form II increases the possibility of arithmetic overflow for filters of high Q or resonance. It has been shown that as Q increases, the round-off noise of both direct form topologies increases without bounds. This is because, conceptually, the signal is first passed through an all-pole filter (which normally boosts gain at the resonant frequencies) before the result of that is saturated, then passed through an all-zero filter (which often attenuates much of what the all-pole half amplifies).

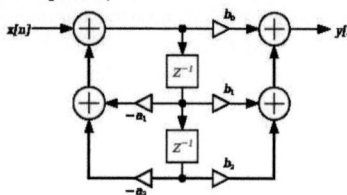

Cascaded second-order sections

A common strategy is to realize a higher-order (greater than 2) digital filter as a cascaded series of second-order "biquadratric" (or "biquad") sections (see digital biquad filter). Advantages of this strategy is that the coefficient range is limited. Cascading direct form II sections result in N delay elements for filter order of N. Cascading direct form I sections result in N+2 delay elements since the delay elements of the input of any section (except the first section) are a redundant with the delay elements of the output of the preceding section.

Other Forms

Other forms include:
Direct Form I and II transpose
Series/cascade lower (typical second) order subsections
Parallel lower (typical second) order subsections
Continued fraction expansion
Lattice and ladder
One, two and three-multiply lattice forms
Three and four-multiply normalized ladder forms
ARMA structures
State-space structures:

optimal (in the minimum noise sense): $(N+1)^2$ parameters
block-optimal and section-optimal: $4N-1$ parameters
input balanced with Givens rotation: $4N-1$ parameters
Coupled forms: Gold Rader (normal), State Variable (Chamberlin), Kingsbury, Modified State Variable, Zölzer, Modified Zölzer
Wave Digital Filters (WDF)
Agarwal-Burrus (1AB and 2AB)
Harris-Brooking
ND-TDL
Multifeedback
Analog-inspired forms such as Sallen-key and state variable filters
Systolic arrays

Comparison of analog and digital filters

Digital filters are not subject to the component non-linearities that greatly complicate the design of analog filters. Analog filters consist of imperfect electronic components, whose values are specified to a limit tolerance (e.g. resistor values often have a tolerance of +/- 5%) and which may also change with temperature and drift with time. As the order of an analog filter increases, and thus its component count, the effect of variable component errors is greatly magnified. In digital filters, the coefficient values are stored in computer memory, making them far more stable and predictable.

Because the coefficients of digital filters are definite, they can be used to achieve much more complex and selective designs – specifically with digital filters, one can achieve a lower passband ripple, faster transition, and higher stopband attenuation than is practical with analog filters. Even if the design could be achieved using analog filters, the engineering cost of designing an equivalent digital filter would likely be much lower. Furthermore, one can readily modify the coefficients of a digital filter to make an adaptive filter or a user-controllable parametric filter. While these techniques are possible in an analog filter, they are again considerably more difficult.

Digital filters can be used in the design of finite impulse response filters. Analog filters do not have the same capability, because finite impulse response filters require delay elements.

Digital filters rely less on analog circuitry, potentially allowing for a better signal-to-noise ratio. A digital filter will introduce noise to a signal during analog low pass filtering, analog to digital conversion, digital to analog conversion and may introduce digital noise due to quantization. With analog filters, every component is a source of thermal noise (such as Johnson noise), so as the filter complexity grows, so does the noise.

However, digital filters do introduce a higher fundamental latency to the system. In an analog filter, latency is often negligible; strictly speaking it is the time for an electrical signal to propagate through the filter circuit. In digital filters, latency is a function of the number of delay elements in the system.

Digital filters also tend to be more limited in bandwidth than analog filters. High bandwidth digital filters require expensive ADC/DACs and fast computer hardware for processing.

In very simple cases, it is more cost effective to use an analog filter. Introducing a digital filter requires considerable overhead circuitry, as previously discussed, including two low pass analog filters.

Types of digital filters

Many digital filters are based on the Fast Fourier transform, a mathematical algorithm that quickly extracts the frequency spectrum of a signal, allowing the spectrum to be manipulated (such as to create band-pass filters) before converting the modified spectrum back into a time-series signal.

Another form of a digital filter is that of a state-space model. A well used state-space filter is the Kalman filter published by Rudolf Kalman in 1960.

Source http://en.wikipedia.org/wiki/Digital_filter

High-pass filter

A **high-pass filter** (HPF) is an electronic filter that passes high-frequency signals but attenuates (reduces the amplitude of) signals with frequencies lower than the cutoff frequency. The actual amount of attenuation for each frequency varies from filter to filter. A high-pass filter is usually modeled as a linear time-invariant system. It is sometimes called a **low-cut filter** or **bass-cut filter**. High-pass filters have many uses, such as blocking DC from circuitry sensitive to non-zero average voltages or RF devices. They can also be used in conjunction with a low-pass filter to make a bandpass filter.

First-order continuous-time implementation

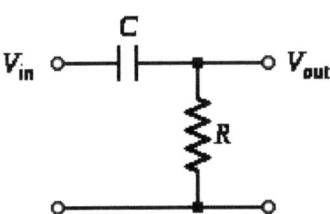

Figure 1: A passive, analog, first-order high-pass filter, realized by an RC circuit

The simple first-order electronic high-pass filter shown in Figure 1 is implemented by placing an input voltage across the series combination of a capacitor and a resistor and using the voltage across the resistor as an output. The product of the resistance and capacitance ($R \times C$) is the time constant (τ); it is inversely proportional to the cutoff frequency f, that is,

$$f_c = \frac{1}{2\pi\tau} = \frac{1}{2\pi RC},$$

where f is in hertz, τ is in seconds, R is in ohms, and C is in farads.

Figure 2 shows an active electronic implementation of a first-order high-pass filter using an operational amplifier. In this case, the filter has a passband gain of -R/R and has a corner frequency of

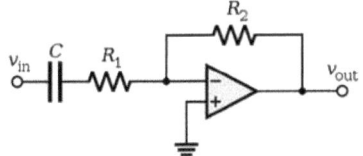

Figure 2: An active high-pass filter

$$f_c = \frac{1}{2\pi\tau} = \frac{1}{2\pi R_1 C},$$

Because this filter is active, it may have non-unity passband gain. That is, high-frequency signals are inverted and amplified by R/R.

Discrete-time realization

Discrete-time high-pass filters can also be designed. Discrete-time filter design is beyond the scope of this article; however, a simple example comes from the conversion of the continuous-time high-pass filter above to a discrete-time realization. That is, the continuous-time behavior can be discretized.

From the circuit in Figure 1 above, according to Kirchhoff's Laws and the definition of capacitance:

$$\begin{cases} V_{\text{out}}(t) = I(t)\,R & \text{(V)} \\ Q_c(t) = C\,(V_{\text{in}}(t) - V_{\text{out}}(t)) & \text{(Q)} \\ I(t) = \frac{dQ_c}{dt} & \text{(I)} \end{cases}$$

where $Q_c(t)$ is the charge stored in the capacitor at time t. Substituting Equation (Q) into Equation (I) and then Equation (I) into Equation (V) gives:

$$V_{\text{out}}(t) = \overbrace{C\left(\frac{dV_{\text{in}}}{dt} - \frac{dV_{\text{out}}}{dt}\right)}^{I(t)} R = RC\left(\frac{dV_{\text{in}}}{dt} - \frac{dV_{\text{out}}}{dt}\right)$$

This equation can be discretized. For simplicity, assume that samples of the input and output are taken at evenly-spaced points in time separated by Δ_T time. Let the samples of V_{in} be represented by the sequence $(x_1, x_2, \ldots, x_n)$, and let V_{out} be represented by the sequence $(y_1, y_2, \ldots, y_n)$ which correspond to the same points in time. Making these substitutions:

$$y_i = RC\left(\frac{x_i - x_{i-1}}{\Delta_T} - \frac{y_i - y_{i-1}}{\Delta_T}\right)$$

And rearranging terms gives the recurrence relation

$$y_i = \overbrace{\frac{RC}{RC + \Delta_T}y_{i-1}}^{\text{Decaying contribution from prior inputs}} + \overbrace{\frac{RC}{RC + \Delta_T}(x_i - x_{i-1})}^{\text{Contribution from change in input}}$$

That is, this discrete-time implementation of a simple continuous-time RC high-pass filter is

$$y_i = \alpha y_{i-1} + \alpha(x_i - x_{i-1}) \quad \text{where} \quad \alpha \triangleq \frac{RC}{RC + \Delta_T}$$

By definition, $0 \leq \alpha \leq 1$. The expression for parameter α yields the equivalent time constant RC in terms of the sampling period Δ_T and α:

$$RC = \Delta_T\left(\frac{\alpha}{1-\alpha}\right)$$

If $\alpha = 0.5$, then the RC time constant equal to the sampling period. If $\alpha \ll 0.5$, then RC is significantly smaller than the sampling interval, and $RC \approx \alpha\Delta_T$.

Algorithmic implementation

The filter recurrence relation provides a way to determine the output samples in terms of the input samples and the preceding output. The following pseudocode algorithm will simulate the effect of a high-pass filter on a series of digital samples:

```
// Return RC high-pass filter output
samples, given input samples,
// time interval dt, and time constant
RC
function highpass(real[0..n] x, real
dt, real RC)
    var real[0..n] y
    var real α := RC / (RC + dt)
    y := x
    for i from 1 to n
        y[i] := α * y[i-1] + α * (x[i] - x[i-1])
    return y
```

The loop which calculates each of the n outputs can be refactored into the equivalent:

```
for i from 1 to n
    y[i] := α * (y[i-1] + x[i] - x[i-1])
```

However, the earlier form shows how the parameter α changes the impact of the prior output y[i-1] and current *change* in input (x[i] - x[i-1]). In particular,

A large α implies that the output will decay very slowly but will also be strongly influenced by even small changes in input. By the relationship between parameter α and time constant RC above, a large α corresponds to a large RC and therefore a low corner frequency of the filter. Hence, this case corresponds to a high-pass filter with a very narrow stop band. Because it is excited by small changes and tends to hold its prior output values for a long time, it can pass relatively low frequencies. However, a constant input (i.e., an input with (x[i] - x[i-1])=0) will always decay to zero, as would be expected with a high-pass filter with a large RC.

A small α implies that the output will decay quickly and will require large changes in the input (i.e., (x[i] - x[i-1]) is large) to cause the output to change much. By the relationship between parameter α and time constant RC above, a small α corresponds to a small RC and therefore a high corner frequency of the filter. Hence, this case corresponds to a high-pass filter with a very wide stop band. Because it requires large (i.e., fast) changes and tends to quickly forget its prior output values, it can only pass relatively high frequencies, as would be expected with a high-pass filter with a small RC.

Applications

Audio

High-pass filters have many applications. They are used as part of an audio crossover to direct high frequencies to a tweeter while attenuating bass signals which could interfere with, or damage, the speaker. When such a filter is built into a loudspeaker cabinet it is normally a passive filter that also includes a low-pass filter for the woofer and so often employs both a capacitor and inductor (although very simple high-pass filters for tweeters can consist of a series capacitor and nothing else). As an example, the formula above, applied to a tweeter with R=10 Ohm, will determine the capacitor value for a cut-off frequency of 5 KHz.

$$C = \frac{1}{2\pi fR} = \frac{1}{6.28 * 5000 * 10} = 3.18 * 10^{-6}$$

, or approx 3.2 µF.

An alternative, which provides good quality sound without inductors (which are prone to parasitic coupling, are expensive, and may have significant internal resistance) is to employ bi-amplification with active RC filters or active digital filters with separate power amplifiers for each loudspeaker. Such low-current and low-voltage line level crossovers are called active crossovers.

Rumble filters are high-pass filters applied to the removal of unwanted sounds near to the lower end of the audible range or below. For example, noises (e.g., footsteps, or motor noises from record players and tape decks) may be removed because they are undesired or may overload the RIAA equalization circuit of the preamp.

High-pass filters are also used for AC coupling at the inputs of many audio power amplifiers, for preventing the amplification of DC currents which may harm the amplifier, rob the amplifier of headroom, and generate waste heat at the loudspeakers voice coil. One amplifier, the professional audio model DC300 made by Crown International beginning in the 1960s, did not have high-pass filtering at all, and could be used to amplify the DC signal of a common 9-volt battery at the input to supply 18 volts DC in an emergency for mixing console power. However, that model's basic design has been superseded by newer designs such as the Crown Macro-Tech series developed in the late 1980s which included 10 Hz high-pass filtering on the inputs and switchable 35 Hz high-pass filtering on the outputs. Another example is the QSC Audio PLX amplifier series which includes an internal 5 Hz high-pass filter which is applied to the inputs whenever the optional 50 and 30 Hz high-pass filters are turned off.

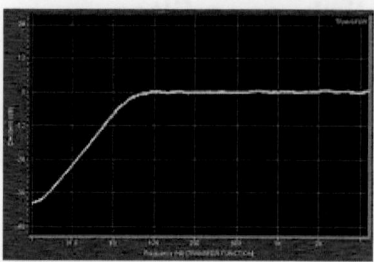

A 75 Hz "low cut" filter from an input channel of a Mackie 1402 mixing console as measured by Smaart software. This high-pass filter has a slope of 18 dB per octave.

Mixing consoles often include high-pass filtering at each channel strip. Some models have fixed-slope, fixed-frequency high-pass filters at 80 or 100 Hz that can be engaged; other models have 'sweepable HPF'—a high-pass filter of fixed slope that can be set within a specified frequency range, such as from 20 to 400 Hz on the Midas Heritage 3000, or 20 to 20,000 Hz on the Yamaha M7CL digital mixing console. Veteran systems engineer and live sound mixer Bruce Main recommends that high-pass filters be engaged for most mixer input sources, except for those such as kick drum, bass guitar and piano, sources which will have useful low frequency sounds. Main writes that DI unit inputs (as opposed to microphone inputs) do not need high-pass filtering as they are not subject to modulation by low-frequency stage wash—low frequency sounds coming from the subwoofers or the public address system and wrapping around to the stage. Main indicates that high-pass filters are commonly used for directional microphones which have a proximity effect—a low-frequency boost for very close sources. This low frequency boost commonly causes problems up to 200 or 300 Hz, but Main notes that he has seen microphones that benefit from a 500 Hz HPF setting on the console.

Image

High-pass and low-pass filters are also used in digital image processing to perform image modifications, enhancements, noise reduction, etc., using de-

Example of high-pass filter applied to the right half of a photograph. Left side is unmodified, Right side is with a high-pass filter applied (in this case, with a radius of 4.9)

signs done in either the spatial domain or the frequency domain.

A high-pass filter, if the imaging software does not have one, can be done by duplicating the layer, putting a gaussian blur, inverting, and then blending with the original layer using an opacity (say 50%) with the original layer.

The unsharp masking, or sharpening, operation used in image editing software is a high-boost filter, a generalization of high-pass.

Source http://en.wikipedia.org/wiki/High-pass_filter

Low-frequency oscillation

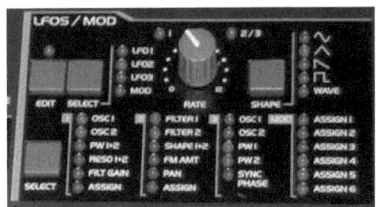

LFO section of a modern synthesizer

Low-frequency oscillation (LFO) is an electronic signal, which is usually below 20 Hz and creates a rhythmic pulse or sweep. This pulse or sweep is often used to modulate synthesizers, delay lines and other audio equipment in order to create effects used in the production of electronic music. Audio effects such as vibrato, tremolo and phasing are examples. The abbreviation is also very often used to refer to **low-frequency oscillators** themselves.

History

Low-frequency oscillation as a concept was first introduced in the modular synths of the 1960s and 70s. Often the LFO effect was accidental; so there were a myriad of configurations that could be 'patched' by the synth operator. LFOs have since appeared in some form on almost every synthesizer. More recently other electronic musical instruments, such as samplers and software synthesizers, have included LFOs to increase their sound alteration capabilities.

Overview

The primary oscillator circuits of a synthesizer are used to create the audio signals. An LFO is a secondary oscillator that operates at a significantly lower frequency (hence its name), typically below 20 Hz. This lower frequency or control signal is used to modulate another component's value, changing the sound without introducing another source. Like a standard oscillator, this usually takes the form of a periodic waveform, such as a sine, sawtooth, triangle or square wave. Also like a standard oscillator, LFOs can incorporate any number of waveform types, including user-defined wavetables, rectified waves and random signals.

Using a low-frequency oscillation signal as a means of modulating another signal introduces complexities into the resulting sound, such that a variety of effects can be achieved. The specifics vary greatly depending on the type of modulation, the relative frequencies of the LFO signal and the signal being modulated, et cetera.

Uses

An LFO can be routed to control, for example, the frequency of the audio oscillator, its phase, stereo panning, filter frequency, or amplification. When routed to control pitch, an LFO creates vibrato. When an LFO modulates amplitude (volume), it creates tremolo. On most synthesizers and sound modules, LFOs feature several controllable parameters, which often include a variety of different waveforms, a rate control, routing options (as described above), a tempo sync feature, and an option to control how much the LFO will modulate the audio signal. LFOs can also be summed and set to different frequencies to create continuously changing slow moving waveforms, and when linked to multiple parameters of a sound, can give the impression that the sound is "alive". An example of software that supports summing LFOs is Evolvor.

Electronic musicians use LFO for a variety of applications. They may be used to add simple vibrato or tremolo to a melody, or for more complex applications such as triggering gate envelopes, or controlling the rate of arpeggiation.

Differences between LFO rates also account for a number of commonly heard effects in modern music. A very low rate can be used to modulate a filter's cutoff frequency, thereby providing the characteristic gradual sensation of the sound becoming clearer or closer to the listener. Alternatively, a high rate can be used for bizarre 'rippling' sound effects (indeed, another important use of LFO is for various sound effects used in films). Dubstep and drum and bass are forms of electronic music which employs frequent use of LFOs, often synchronized to the tempo of the track, for bass sounds that have a "wobble" effect, for example by modulating the cutoff frequency of a low-pass filter to create a distinctive opening-and-closing effect. Due to the popularization of these genres, the LFO wobble is now being found in other forms of electronic dance music such as house music.

Other notes

The British electronic music group LFO take their name directly from the low-frequency oscillator.

Source http://en.wikipedia.org/wiki/Low-frequency_oscillation

Low-pass filter

A **low-pass filter** is an electronic filter that passes low-frequency signals and attenuates (reduces the amplitude of) signals with frequencies higher than the cutoff frequency. The actual amount of attenuation for each frequency varies from filter to filter. It is sometimes called a **high-cut filter**, or **treble cut filter** when used in audio applications. A low-pass filter is the opposite of a high-pass filter. A band-pass filter is a combination of a low-pass and a high-pass.

Low-pass filters exist in many different forms, including electronic circuits (such as a *hiss filter* used in audio), anti-aliasing filters for conditioning signals prior to analog-to-digital conversion, digital filters for smoothing sets of data, acoustic barriers, blurring of images, and so on. The moving average operation used in fields such as finance is a particular kind of low-pass filter, and can be analyzed with the same signal processing techniques as are used for other low-pass filters. Low-pass filters provide a smoother form of a signal, removing the short-term fluctuations, and leaving the longer-term trend.

An optical filter could correctly be called low-pass, but conventionally is described as "longpass" (low frequency is long wavelength), to avoid confusion.

Examples of low-pass filters

Acoustic

A stiff physical barrier tends to reflect higher sound frequencies, and so acts as a low-pass filter for transmitting sound. When music is playing in another room, the low notes are easily heard, while the high notes are attenuated.

Electronic

In an electronic low-pass RC filter for voltage signals, high frequencies contained in the input signal are attenuated but the filter has little attenuation below its cutoff frequency which is determined by its RC time constant.

For current signals, a similar circuit using a resistor and capacitor in parallel works in a similar manner. See current divider discussed in more detail below.

Electronic low-pass filters are used on input signals to subwoofers and other types of loudspeakers, to block high pitches that they can't efficiently reproduce.

Radio transmitters use low-pass filters to block harmonic emissions which might cause interference with other communications.

The tone knob found on many electric guitars is a low-pass filter used to reduce the amount of treble in the sound.

An integrator is another example of a single time constant low-pass filter.

Telephone lines fitted with DSL splitters use low-pass and high-pass filters to separate DSL and POTS signals sharing the same pair of wires.

Low-pass filters also play a significant role in the sculpting of sound for electronic music as created by analogue synthesisers. *See subtractive synthesis.*

Ideal and real filters

An ideal low-pass filter completely eliminates all frequencies above the cutoff frequency while passing those below unchanged; its frequency response is a rectangular function and is a brick-wall filter. The transition region present in practical filters does not exist in an ideal filter. An ideal low-pass filter can be realized mathematically (theoretical-

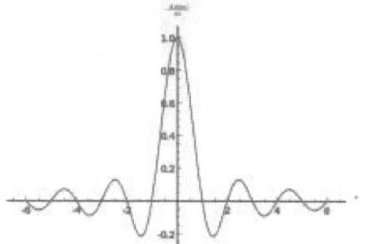

The sinc function, the impulse response of an ideal low-pass filter.

ly) by multiplying a signal by the rectangular function in the frequency domain or, equivalently, convolution with its impulse response, a sinc function, in the time domain.

However, the ideal filter is impossible to realize without also having signals of infinite extent in time, and so generally needs to be approximated for real ongoing signals, because the sinc function's support region extends to all past and future times. The filter would therefore need to have infinite delay, or knowledge of the infinite future and past, in order to perform the convolution. It is effectively realizable for pre-recorded digital signals by assuming extensions of zero into the past and future, or more typically by making the signal repetitive and using Fourier analysis.

Real filters for real-time applications approximate the ideal filter by truncating and windowing the infinite impulse response to make a finite impulse response; applying that filter requires delaying the signal for a moderate period of time, allowing the computation to "see" a little bit into the future. This delay is manifested as phase shift. Greater accuracy in approximation requires a longer delay.

An ideal low-pass filter results in

ringing artifacts via the Gibbs phenomenon. These can be reduced or worsened by choice of windowing function, and the design and choice of real filters involves understanding and minimizing these artifacts. For example, "simple truncation [of sinc] causes severe ringing artifacts," in signal reconstruction, and to reduce these artifacts one uses window functions "which drop off more smoothly at the edges."

The Whittaker–Shannon interpolation formula describes how to use a perfect low-pass filter to reconstruct a continuous signal from a sampled digital signal. Real digital-to-analog converters use real filter approximations.

Continuous-time low-pass filters

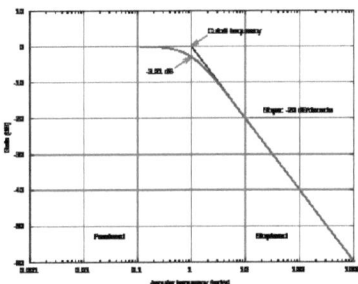

The gain-magnitude frequency response of a first-order (one-pole) low-pass filter. *Power gain* is shown in decibels (i.e., a 3 dB decline reflects an additional half-power attenuation). Angular frequency is shown on a logarithmic scale in units of radians per second.

There are many different types of filter circuits, with different responses to changing frequency. The frequency response of a filter is generally represented using a Bode plot, and the filter is characterized by its cutoff frequency and rate of frequency rolloff. In all cases, at the *cutoff frequency*, the filter attenuates the input power by half or 3 dB. So the **order** of the filter determines the amount of additional attenuation for frequencies higher than the cutoff frequency.

A **first-order filter**, for example, will reduce the signal amplitude by half (so power reduces by a factor of 4), or 6 dB, every time the frequency doubles (goes up one octave); more precisely, the power rolloff approaches 20 dB per decade in the limit of high frequency. The magnitude Bode plot for a first-order filter looks like a horizontal line below the cutoff frequency, and a diagonal line above the cutoff frequency. There is also a "knee curve" at the boundary between the two, which smoothly transitions between the two straight line regions. If the transfer function of a first-order low-pass filter has a zero as well as a pole, the Bode plot will flatten out again, at some maximum attenuation of high frequencies; such an effect is caused for example by a little bit of the input leaking around the one-pole filter; this one-pole–one-zero filter is still a first-order low-pass. *See Pole–zero plot and RC circuit.*

A **second-order filter** attenuates higher frequencies more steeply. The Bode plot for this type of filter resembles that of a first-order filter, except that it falls off more quickly. For example, a second-order Butterworth filter will reduce the signal amplitude to one fourth its original level every time the frequency doubles (so power decreases by 12 dB per octave, or 40 dB per decade). Other all-pole second-order filters may roll off at different rates initially depending on their Q factor, but approach the same final rate of 12 dB per octave; as with the first-order filters, zeroes in the transfer function can change the high-frequency asymptote. See RLC circuit.

Third- and higher-order filters are defined similarly. In general, the final rate of power rolloff for an order-n all-pole filter is $6n$ dB per octave (i.e., $20n$ dB per decade).

On any Butterworth filter, if one extends the horizontal line to the right and the diagonal line to the upper-left (the asymptotes of the function), they will intersect at exactly the "cutoff frequency". The frequency response at the cutoff frequency in a first-order filter is 3 dB below the horizontal line. The various types of filters (Butterworth filter, Chebyshev filter, Bessel filter, etc.) all have different-looking "knee curves". Many second-order filters are designed to have "peaking" or resonance, causing their frequency response at the cutoff frequency to be *above* the horizontal line. Furthermore, the actual frequency at which this peaking occurs can be predicted without calculus, as shown by Cartwright et al. *See electronic filter for other types.*

The meanings of 'low' and 'high' – that is, the cutoff frequency – depend on the characteristics of the filter. The term "low-pass filter" merely refers to the shape of the filter's response; a high-pass filter could be built that cuts off at a lower frequency than any low-pass filter—it is their responses that set them apart. Electronic circuits can be devised for any desired frequency range, right up through microwave frequencies (above 1 GHz) and higher.

Laplace notation

Continuous-time filters can also be described in terms of the Laplace transform of their impulse response in a way that allows all of the characteristics of the filter to be easily analyzed by considering the pattern of poles and zeros of the Laplace transform in the complex plane (in discrete time, one can similarly consider the Z-transform of the impulse response).

For example, a first-order low-pass filter can be described in Laplace notation as

$$\frac{\text{Output}}{\text{Input}} = K \frac{1}{1 + s\tau}$$

where s is the Laplace transform variable, τ is the filter time constant, and K is the filter passband gain.

Electronic low-pass filters

Passive electronic realization

One simple electrical circuit that will serve as a low-pass filter consists of a resistor in series with a load, and a capacitor in parallel with the load. The capacitor exhibits reactance, and blocks low-frequency signals, causing them to go through the load instead. At higher frequencies the reactance drops, and the capacitor effectively functions as a short circuit. The combination of resistance and capacitance gives the time constant of the filter $\tau = RC$ (repre-

Low-pass filter

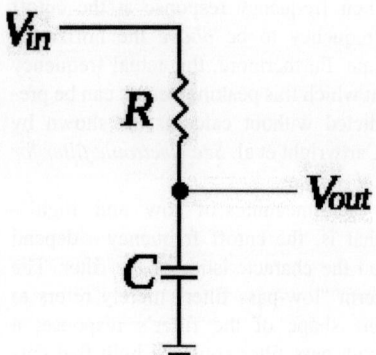

Passive, first order low-pass RC filter

sented by the Greek letter tau). The break frequency, also called the turnover frequency or cutoff frequency (in hertz), is determined by the time constant:

$$f_c = \frac{1}{2\pi\tau} = \frac{1}{2\pi RC}$$

or equivalently (in radians per second):

$$\omega_c = \frac{1}{\tau} = \frac{1}{RC}$$

One way to understand this circuit is to focus on the time the capacitor takes to charge. It takes time to charge or discharge the capacitor through that resistor:

At low frequencies, there is plenty of time for the capacitor to charge up to practically the same voltage as the input voltage.

At high frequencies, the capacitor only has time to charge up a small amount before the input switches direction. The output goes up and down only a small fraction of the amount the input goes up and down. At double the frequency, there's only time for it to charge up half the amount.

Another way to understand this circuit is with the idea of reactance at a particular frequency:

Since DC cannot flow through the capacitor, DC input must "flow out" the path marked V_{out} (analogous to removing the capacitor).

Since AC flows very well through the capacitor — almost as well as it flows through solid wire — AC input "flows out" through the capacitor, effectively short circuiting to ground (analogous to replacing the capacitor with just a wire). The capacitor is not an "on/off" object (like the block or pass fluidic explanation above). The capacitor will variably act between these two extremes. It is the Bode plot and frequency response that show this variability.

Active electronic realization

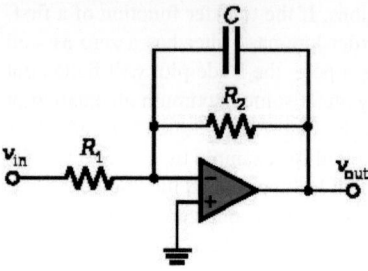

An active low-pass filter

Another type of electrical circuit is an *active* low-pass filter.

In the operational amplifier circuit shown in the figure, the cutoff frequency (in hertz) is defined as:

$$f_c = \frac{1}{2\pi R_2 C}$$

or equivalently (in radians per second):

$$\omega_c = \frac{1}{R_2 C}$$

The gain in the passband is $-R/R$, and the stopband drops off at -6 dB per octave (that is -20 dB per decade) as it is a first-order filter.

Discrete-time realization

Many digital filters are designed to give low-pass characteristics. Both infinite impulse response and finite impulse response low pass filters as well as filters using fourier transforms are widely used.

Simple infinite impulse response filter

The effect of an infinite impulse response low-pass filter can be simulated on a computer by analyzing an RC filter's behavior in the time domain, and then discretizing the model.

From the circuit diagram to the right, according to Kirchhoff's Laws and the

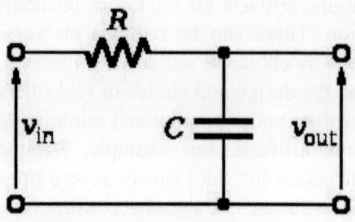

A simple low-pass RC filter

definition of capacitance:

$$v_{\text{in}}(t) - v_{\text{out}}(t) = R\,i(t)$$

$$Q_c(t) = C\,v_{\text{out}}(t)$$

$$i(t) = \frac{d\,Q_c}{d\,t}$$

where $Q_c(t)$ is the charge stored in the capacitor at time t. Substituting equation Q into equation I gives $i(t) = C\frac{d\,v_{\text{out}}}{d\,t}$, which can be substituted into equation V so that:

$$v_{\text{in}}(t) - v_{\text{out}}(t) = RC\frac{d\,v_{\text{out}}}{d\,t}$$

This equation can be discretized. For simplicity, assume that samples of the input and output are taken at evenly-spaced points in time separated by ΔT time. Let the samples of v_{in} be represented by the sequence $(x_1, x_2, ..., x_n)$, and let v_{out} be represented by the sequence $(y_1, y_2, ..., y_n)$ which correspond to the same points in time. Making these substitutions:

$$x_i - y_i = RC\frac{y_i - y_{i-1}}{\Delta_T}$$

And rearranging terms gives the recurrence relation

$$y_i = \overbrace{x_i\left(\frac{\Delta_T}{RC + \Delta_T}\right)}^{\text{Input contribution}} + \overbrace{y_{i-1}\left(\frac{RC}{RC + \Delta_T}\right)}^{\text{Inertia from previous output}}.$$

That is, this discrete-time implementation of a simple RC low-pass filter is the exponentially-weighted moving average

$$y_i = \alpha x_i + (1-\alpha) y_{i-1} \quad \text{where} \quad \alpha \triangleq \frac{\Delta_T}{RC + \Delta_T}$$

By definition, the *smoothing factor* $0 \leq \alpha \leq 1$. The expression for α yields the equivalent time constant RC

in terms of the sampling period Δ_T and smoothing factor α:

$$RC = \Delta_T \left(\frac{1 - \alpha}{\alpha} \right)$$

If $\alpha = 0.5$, then the RC time constant is equal to the sampling period. If $\alpha \ll 0.5$, then RC is significantly larger than the sampling interval, and $\Delta_T \approx \alpha RC$.

The filter recurrence relation provides a way to determine the output samples in terms of the input samples and the preceding output. The following pseudocode algorithm will simulate the effect of a low-pass filter on a series of digital samples:

// Return RC low-pass filter output samples, given input samples,
// time interval *dt*, and time constant *RC*

function lowpass(*real[0..n]* x, *real* dt, *real* RC)
  var *real[0..n]* y
  var *real* α := dt / (RC + dt)
  y := x
  for i **from** 1 **to** n
    y[i] := α * x[i] + (1-α) * y[i-1]
  return y

The loop that calculates each of the *n* outputs can be refactored into the equivalent:

for i **from** 1 **to** n
  y[i] := y[i-1] + α * (x[i] - y[i-1])

That is, the change from one filter output to the next is proportional to the difference between the previous output and the next input. This exponential smoothing property matches the exponential decay seen in the continuous-time system. As expected, as the time constant RC increases, the discrete-time smoothing parameter α decreases, and the output samples $(y_1, y_2, ..., y_n)$ respond more slowly to a change in the input samples $(x_1, x_2, ..., x_n)$; the system will have more *inertia*. This filter is an infinite-impulse-response (IIR) single-pole low-pass filter.

Finite impulse response

Finite impulse response filters can be built that approximate to the ideal sinc time domain response. In practice the time domain response must be time truncated and is often of a simplified shape; in the simplest case, a running average can be used giving a square time response.

Source http://en.wikipedia.org/wiki/Low-pass_filter

Music sequencer

A **music sequencer** (or simply **sequencer**) is a device or application software that can record, edit, or play back music, by handling note and performance information in several forms, typically MIDI or CV/Gate, and possibly audio and automation data for DAWs and plug-ins.

Overview

Types of music sequencers
As mentioned above, music sequencers are often categorized by handling data types, as following:
MIDI *data* on the **MIDI sequencers** (implemented as hardware or software)
CV/Gate *data* on the **analog sequencers**, and possibly others (via CV/Gate interfaces).
Automation *data* for **DAWs** and **plug-ins**.
on the DAW with sequencing features, and software instrument/effect plug-ins on them.
Audio *data*
on the audio sequencers including **DAW**, loop-based music software, *etc*; or, the phrase samplers including

Groove machines, *etc*.
Also, music sequencer can be categorized by its construction and supporting modes.

Realtime sequencer (realtime recording mode)

A realtime sequencer on the synthesizer

Realtime sequencer records the musical notes in real-time as on audio recorders, and play-back musical notes with designated tempo, quantizations, and pitch. For editing, usually "*punch in/punch out*" feature originated in the tape recording is provided, although it requires enough skills to obtain desired result. For detailed editing, possibly another visual *editing modes* under graphical user interface may be more suitable. Anyway, this mode provides usability similar to the audio recorder already familiarized by musicians, and it is widely supported on software sequencer, DAW, and built-in hardware sequencers.

Analog sequencer

An analog sequencer

Analog sequencers are typically implemented with analog electronics, and play the musical notes designated by a series of knobs or sliders corresponding to each musical note (*step*). It is designed for both composition and live performance; users can anytime change the musical notes without regarding *recording* mode. And also possibly, the time-interval between each musical note (length of each *step*) can be independently adjustable. Typically, analog sequencer is used to generate the *repeated minimalistic phrases* which is reminiscent of Tangerine Dream, Giorgio Moroder or trance music.

Step sequencer (step recording mode)

A step sequencer on the drum machine

On the step sequencers, musical notes are rounded into the *steps* with equal time-interval, and users can enter each musical note without exact timing. Instead, the timing and duration are designated in several ways:
On the bass machines: entering order of steps, and selection of *length-buttons*.
On the drum machines: selection of column of *timing-buttons*
On several home keyboards: individual timing recording in realtime, using *trigger-buttons*
In general, *step* mode, along with *semi-realtime* mode, is often supported on the analog drum machines, bass machines and several groove machines,

Software sequencer
Software sequencer is a class of application software providing a functionality of music sequencer, and often provided as a feature of the DAW or the integrated music authoring environments. The features provided are wide variety depend on each software; even an *analog sequencer* can be simulated on it. The user may control the software sequencer either by using the graphical user interfaces or a specialized input devices, such as a MIDI controller.

Typical features on software sequencers

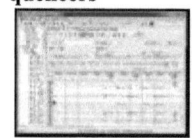 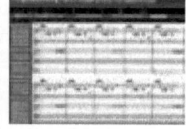

Numerical editor on Tracker   Score editor

Modern sequencers
With the advent of MIDI and particularly Atari ST in 1980s, programmers were able to write software that could record and play back the notes played by a musician. Unlike the early sequencers used to play mechanical sounding sequence with exactly equal length, the new ones recorded and played back expressive performances by real musicians. These were typically used to control external synthesizers, especially rackmounted sound modules as it was no longer necessary for each synthesizer to have its own keyboard.

As the technology matured, sequencers gained more features, and integrated the ability to record multitrack audio. Sequencers mainly used for audio are often called digital audio workstations (or DAWs).

Many modern sequencers can also control virtual instruments implemented as software plug-ins, allowing musicians to replace separate synthesizers with software equivalents.

Today the term "sequencer" is often used to describe software. However, hardware sequencers still exist. Workstation keyboards have their own proprietary built-in MIDI sequencers. Drum machines and some older synthesizers have their own step sequencer built in. There are still also standalone hardware MIDI sequencers, although the market demand for those has diminished greatly due to the greater feature set of their software counterparts.

History

Today's typical software sequencer, supporting multitrack audio (DAW) and plug-ins (Steinberg Cubase 6)

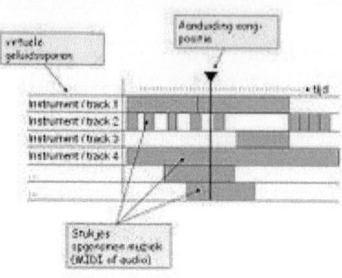

User interface on Steinberg Cubase v6.0, a digital audio workstation with an integrated software sequencer.

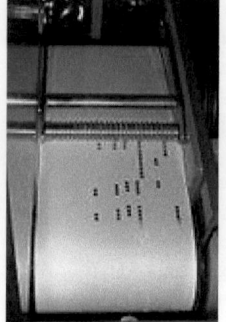

Music roll on barrel organ

Barrel with pins on the large stationary barrel-organ

Early sequencers
The early music sequencers had appeared in the form of various automatic musical instruments, including music boxes, mechanical organs, player pianos, Orchestrions, *etc.* For example, authoring process of piano roll fits the definition of *music sequencer*: composers *record* their music composition on the piano rolls, then specialists *edit* the rolls as the preparation before mass duplication, and finally consumers *play* back the music on their player pianos.

The origin of automatic musical instruments seems considerably old. As early as 9th century, Persian inventors Banū Mūsā brothers invented *hydropowered organ* using exchangeable cylinders with pins, and also *automatic flute player* using steam power, as described on their *Book of Ingenious Devices*. In 14th century, rotating cylinder with pins were used to play carillon in Flanders, and at least in 15th century, barrel organs were seen in the Netherlands.

RCA Mark II (1957), controlled via punch tape

Player piano (1920) controlled by piano roll

In 19th century, as the results of Industrial Revolution, various *automatic musical instruments* were invented, for examples: music box, barrel organ and barrel piano using barrel / cylinder with pins or metal disc with punched holes; or mechanical organ, player piano and orchestrion using book music / music rolls (piano rolls) with punched holes, *etc.* These instruments were widely spread as the popular entertainment devices before the inventions of phonograph, radio, and sound film. Amongst of all, especially the *punched tape media* had been long lived until mid-20th century: earliest programmable music synthesizers including *RCA Mark II Sound Synthesizer* in 1957, and *Siemens Synthesizer* in 1959, were also controlled via punch tapes similar to piano rolls.

Another inventions were came from sound film technology. The drawn sound *technique* which appeared in the late 1920s, is notable as a precursor of today's intuitive graphical user interfaces. On this technique, notes and various sound parameters were controlled by hand-drawn waves on the films, resembling *piano rolls* or *strip charts* on the modern sequencers/DAWs. It was often utilized on early experiments of electronic music, including *Variophone* developed by Yevgeny Sholpo in 1930, and *Oramics* designed by Daphne Oram in 1957, *etc.*

Buchla 250e (2004) seems influenced by *Circle Machine*

Analog sequencers

Moog sequencer module (left, probably added after 1968) on Moog Modular (1964)

One of the earliest commercially available analog sequencers (front) on Buchla 100 (1964/1966)

During 1940s–1960s, Raymond Scott, an American composer of electronic music, invented various kind of music sequencers for his electric compositions. The "*Wall of Sound*", once covered on the wall of his studio in New York during 1940s–1950s, was an electro-mechanical sequencer to produce rhythmic patterns, consisting of stepping relays (used on dial pulse telephone exchange), solenoids, control switches, and tone circuits with 16 individual oscillators. Later, Robert Moog explained it "*the whole room would go 'clack - clack - clack', and the sounds would come out all over the place*". The *Circle Machine*, developed in 1959, had dimmer bulbs arranged in a ring, and a rotating arm with photocell scanning over the ring, to generate arbitrary waveform. Also, the rotating speed of arm was controlled via brightness of lights, and as the results, arbitrary rhythms were generated. And relatively well known *Clavivox*, developed since 1952, was a kind of keyboard synthesizer with sequencer. On its prototype, a theremin manufactured by young Robert Moog was utilized to enable portamento over 3-octave range, and on later version, it was replaced by a pair of photographic film and photocell for controlling the pitch by voltage.

In 1965 Ralph Lundsten had a polyphonic synthesizer with sequencer called Andromatic. built for him by Erkki Kurenniemi.

Step sequencers

Firstman SQ-01 (1980), one of the earliest step bass machines

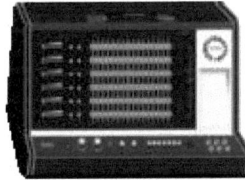

Eko ComputeRhythm (1972), one of the earliest programmable drum machines

The **step sequencer**s played rigid patterns of notes using a grid of (usually) 16 buttons, or steps, each step being 1/

16 of a measure. These patterns of notes were then chained together to form longer compositions. Sequencers of this kind are still in use, mostly built into drum machines and grooveboxes. They are monophonic by nature, although some are multi-timbral, meaning that they can control several different sounds but only play one note on each of those sounds.

Computer music

Max Mathews playing a violin connected to the GROOVE system (1970)

CSIRAC played the earliest computer music in 1951

On the other hand, software sequencers were continuously utilized since 1950s, in the context of *computer music*, including computer *played* music (software sequencer), computer *composed* music (music synthesis), and computer *sound generation* (sound synthesis). In June 1951, first computer music *Colonel Bogey* was *played* on CSIRAC, Australia's first digital computer. In 1956, Lejaren Hiller at University of Illinois at Urbana-Champaign wrote an earliest program for *computer music composition* on ILLIAC, and collaborated on the first piece, *Illiac Suite for String Quartet*, with Leonard Issaction. In 1957, Max Mathews at Bell Labs wrote MUSIC, a first *widely-used* program for *sound generation*, and 17 second composition was performed by the IBM 704 computer. Since then, computer music were mainly researched on the expensive mainframe computers on the computer centers, until 1970s when minicomputers and following microcomputers went into practice on this field.

Digital sequencers

Roland MC-4 (1981), a successor of the MC-8 (1977)

EMS Sequencer 256 (1971), a branched product of the Synthi 100

In 1971, Electronic Music Studios (EMS) released one of the first digital sequencer products as a module of Synthi 100, and separated products Synthi Sequencer *series*. After then, Oberheim released *DS-2 Digital Sequencer* in 1974, and Sequential Circuits released *Model 800* in 1977

Also in 1977, Roland Corporation released their first microcomputer-based digital sequencer, MC-8 Microcomposer, also called *computer music composer* by Roland. It equipped keypad to enter note in numeric code, 16KB RAM for maximum 5200 notes (large enough at that time), and polyphony function which allocates multiple pitch CV into single Gate. The earliest known user was Yellow Magic Orchestra in 1978, an electronic music group.

Software sequencers

In 1975, New England Digital (NED) released *ABLE computer* (microcomputer) as a dedicated data processing unit for *Dartmouth Digital Synthesizer* (1973), and based on it, later Synclavier series were developed. The *Synclavier*

Fairlight CMI (1979)

Synclavier I (1977)

I, released in September 1977, was one of the earliest digital music workstation product with multitrack sequencer. Synclavier series evolved throughout late 1970s–mid-1980s, and they also established integration of digital-audio and *music-sequencer*, on their *Direct-to-Disk* option in 1984, and later *Tapeless Studio* system.

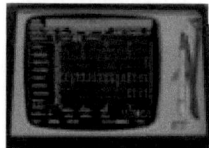

Page R on Fairlight

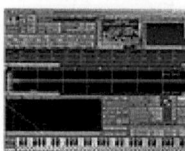

Tracker software

In 1980, renewed Fairlight CMI *Series II* with its sequencer, "*Page R*", combined step sequencing with sample playback. In 1987, this led to the development of similar software sequencers of this kind, called **Trackers**, which became popular in the 1980s and 1990s as simple sequencers for creating computer game music, and are yet popular in the Demoscene and Chiptunes.

Visual timeline of rhythm sequencers

Mechanical (pre 20c)   Rhythmicon (1930)

Hardware sequencers

Many synthesizers, and by definition all music workstations, groove machines and drum machines, contain their own sequencers.

Followings are **specifically designed to function primarily as the music sequencers**:

Rotating object with pins or holes

Barrel or cylinder with pins (since 9th or 14th century) utilized on barrel organs, carillons, music boxes
Metal disc with punched holes (late 1800s) — utilized on several music boxes such as *Polyphon, Regina, Symphonion, Ariston, Graphonola* (early version), *etc.*

Punched paper

Book music (since 1890) utilized on several mechanical organs
Music roll utilized on player pianos (using piano rolls), Orchestrions, several mechanical organs, *etc.*
Punch tape system for earliest studio synthesizers
RCA Mark II Sound Synthesizer (1957) by Herbert Belar and Harry Olson at RCA
Room-filling device built in 1957 for half a million dollars. Included a 4-polyphony synth with 12 oscillators, a sequencer fed with wide paper tape, and output were recorded on a shellac record lathe.
Siemens Synthesizer (1959)

Sound-on-film

Oramics (1957) controls sounds by graphics on films

Variophone (1930) by Evgeny Sholpo — on earliest version, hand drawn waves on film or disc were used to synthesize sound, and later versions were promised to experiment on musical intonations and temporal characteristics of live music performance, however not finished. Variophone is often referred as a forerunner of drawn sound system including *ANS synthesizer* and *Oramics*.
Composer-Tron (1953) by Osmond Kendal — rhythmical sequences were controlled via marking cue on film, while timbre of note or envelope-shape of sound were defined via hand drawn shapes on a surface of CRT input device, drawn with a grease pencil.
ANS synthesizer (1938-1958) by Evgeny Murzin — An earliest realtime additive synthesizer using 720 microtonal sine waves (1/6 semitones × 10 octaves) generated by five glas discs. Composers could control time evolution of amplitudes of each microtones via scratches on glass plate user interface covered with black mastic.
Oramics (1957) by Daphne Oram — hand drawn contours on a set of ten sprocketed synchronized strips of 35 film were used to control various parameters of monophonic sound generator (frequency, timbre, amplitude and duration). Polyphonic sounds were obtained using multitrack recording technique.

Electro-mechanical sequencers

Wall of Sound (mid-1940s–1950s) by Raymond Scott — early electro-mechanical sequencer developed by Raymond Scott to produce rhythmic patterns, consistead with stepping relays, solenoids, and tone generators.
Circle Machine (1959) by Raymond

Wurlitzer Sideman (1959)

Scott — electro-optical rotary sequencer developed by Raymond Scott to generate arbitrary waveforms, consisted with dimmer bulbs arranged in a ring, and a rotating arm with photocell scanning over the ring.
Wurlitzer Sideman (1959) — first commercial drum machine; rhythm patterns were electro-mechanically generated by rotating disk switches, and drum sounds were electronically generated by vacuum-tube circuits.

Analog sequencers

Analog sequencers with CV/Gate interface

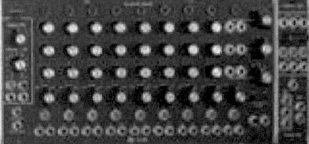

Moog 960 Sequential Controller and 962 Sequential Switch

Buchla 100's sequencer modules (1964/1966–) — One of the earliest analog sequencer on the modular synthesizer era since 1960. Later, Robert Moog admired Buchla's unique works including it.
Moog 960 Sequential Controller / 961 Interface / 962 Sequential Switch (c. 1968)
modules for the Moog modular synthesizer system, a popular analog sequencer following earliest Buchla sequencer.

Doepfer Dark Time
genoQs Octopus
genoQs Nemo

Serge Modular TKB Synthesizers.

Korg SQ-10
MFB Urzwerg / MFB Urzwerg Pro — *CV/Gate step sequencer with 8steps/4tracks or 16steps/2tracks; also synchronizable with MIDI sequencer*

com Q119 Synthesizers. com Q960 — *reissue of Moog 960*

Yamaha CS30 (1977) — *monophonic synthesizer keyboard with built-in 8-step analog sequencer*

Analog-style step sequencers
Analog-style MIDI step sequencers
Since the analog synthesizer revivals in 1990s, newly designed MIDI sequencers with a series of knobs or slider similar to analog sequencer have been appeared. These often equip CV/Gate and DIN sync interface along with MIDI, and even the patch memory for multiple sequence patterns and possibly song sequence. These analog-digital hybrid machines are often called *Analog-style MIDI step sequencer* or *MIDI analog sequencer*, etc.

Quasimidi Polymorph (1999) has built-in step sequencer with a series of value knobs (bottom)

Doepfer MAQ 16/3 — *MIDI analog sequencer, designed in cooperation with Kraftwerk*
Doepfer Regelwerk — *MIDI analog sequencer with MIDI controller*
Frostwave Fat Controller
Infection Music Phaedra
Infection Music Zeit
Latronic Notron
Manikin Schrittmacher
Quasimidi Polymorph (1999) — *Four-part multitimbral tabletop synthesizer, with an analog-like step sequencer.*
Roland EF-303 – *Multiple effects unit with 16-step modulation, also usable as the analog-style MIDI step sequencer.*
Sequentix P3

Analog-style MIDI pattern sequencers
Several machines also provide the *song mode* to play the sequence of memoried patterns in specified order, as on drum machine.
Doepfer Schaltwerk —*MIDI pattern sequencer*

Step sequencers (supported on)
Typical step sequencers are integrated on drum machines, bass machines, groove machines, music production machines, and these software versions. Often, these also support the *semi-realtime* recording mode, too.
MFB Step 64 — *Standalone step sequencer dedicated for drum patterns (16steps/4tracks or 64steps/1tracks, 118program×4banks, 16song sequences, each with up to 128 sequences)*

Casio VL-Tone VL-1

Casio Sampletone SK-1

Embedded self-contained step sequencers
Several tiny keyboards provide a step sequencer combined with realtime recording mode dedicated for timings:
Casio VL-Tone VL-1 (1979), Casiotone MT-70 (c.1984), Sampletone SK-1 (1986), etc — *Timings of musical notes stored on the step sequencer, can be designated by the two trigger buttons labeled "One Key Play", around the right hand position.*

Embedded CV/Gate step sequencers
Several machines have white & black chromatic keypads, to enter the musical phrases.
Multivox / Firstman SQ-01 (1980) — *a forerunner of TB-303*
Roland TB-303 (1981)
Roland SH-101 (1982) — *monophonic keytar synthesizer with sequencer*
Roland MC-202 (1983) — *monophonic tabletop synthesizer with sequencer, similar to MC-101*

Embedded MIDI step sequencers
Groovebox-type machines with white & black chromatic keypads, often support *step recording* mode along with *realtime recording* mode:

Korg Electribe *series*
Roland Corporation MC *series: MC-09 / MC-303 / MC-505 / MC-808 / MC-909*

Yamaha RM1x
Yamaha RS7000 — *Music Production Studio*

Other groovebox-type machines (including several music production machines) also often support step recording mode, of course:

Linn 9000 (1984)
Sequential Circuits Studio 440 (1986)
E-mu SP-12 (1986)
E-mu SP-1200 (1987)
Akai MPC series (1988–)

Akai MPC Renaissance / Studio / Fly (2012) — *Software with control surfaces*
Native Instruments Maschine (2009) — *Software with control surface*
Roland MV-30
Roland MV-8000 — *Production Studio*

Button-grid-style step sequencers
Recently emerging *button-grid*-style interfaces/instruments are naturally support step sequence. On these machines, one axis on grid means musical scale, and another axis means timing of notes.

Tenori-on

Akai APC40 — interface for Ableton Live
Arduinome — interface
Bliptronics 5000 — instrument
Monome — interface

Novation Launchpad — interface for Ableton Live

Yamaha Tenori-on — instrument

In addition, newly designed hardware MIDI sequencers equipping a series of knobs/sliders similar to analog sequencers, are appeared. For details, see #Analog-style MIDI step sequencers.

Digital sequencers

CV/Gate

Also often support Gate clock and DIN sync interfaces.

EDP Spider (late 1970s) — *supported LINK and CV/Gate*

EMS Sequencer *series* (1971)

Max Mathews GROOVE *system* (1970)

Multivox MX-8100 / Firstman SQ-10 (1979/1980) — *supported V/Oct. and Hz/V*

Oberheim DS-2 (1974)

Roland CSQ-100

Roland CSQ-600 (1980) — *it memories 600 notes for individual 4 tracks, a buddy of TR-808*

Roland MC-4 Microcomposer (1981)

Roland MC-8 Microcomposer (1977) — *also supporting DCB via OP-8*

Sequential Circuits Model 800 (1977)

Proprietary digital interfaces (pre MIDI era)

NED Synclavier *series* — CV/Gate interface and MIDI retrofit kit were available on Synclavier II. Also MIDI became standard feature on Synclavier PSMT.

Fairlight CMI *series* — CV/Gate interface was optionally available on Series II, and MIDI was supported on Series IIx and later models.

Oberheim DSX (Oberheim Parallel Bus)

PPG Wave *family* (PPG Bus)

Rhodes Chroma (Chroma Computer Interface)

Roland JSQ-60 (Roland Digital Control Bus (DCB))

Sequential Circuits PolySequencer 1005 (SCI Serial Bus)

Yamaha CS70M (Key Code Interface)

MIDI sequencers

Standalone MIDI sequencers

Akai ASQ10

Alesis MMT-8 — *a buddy of HR-16 drum machine*

Korg SQD-1

Korg SQD-8

Kawai Q-80

Roland MC-327

Roland MC *series*: MC-50/MC-50MkII/MC-80/MC-300/MC-500 Microcomposer

Roland MSQ-100 (1985)

Roland MSQ-700 (1984) — one of the earliest multitrack MIDI sequencer (8tr), a buddy of TR-909

Roland SB-55 — *SMF recorder*

Yamaha QX *series*: QX1/QX3/QX5/QX7/QX21

MIDI phrase sequencers

Zyklus MPS

MIDI sequencers with embedded sound module

Yamaha QY300 — *with embedded sound module*

Yamaha QY700 — *with embedded sound module*

Palmtop MIDI sequencers

Yamaha QY10

Korg SQ-8 — *palmtop sequencer*

Philips Micro Composer PMC100

Roland PMA-5 — *palmtop sequencer with touch screen*

Yamaha Walkstation series: MU5/MU10/MU15/QY8/QY10/QY20/(— *palmtop sequencer with embedded sound module.*

Accompaniment machines

Yamaha QR10

Open-source hardware

Rebeltech Stoicheia — Gate sequencer generating Euclidean Rhythm

MIDIbox Sequencer modules — Analog-style MIDI step sequencer/MIDI effect processor modules of MIDIbox project

Software sequencers / DAWs with sequencing features

Free/Open Source

MIDI sequencers

Aria Maestosa - Windows, Linux, Mac

BRELS Midi Editor - Windows

Edge - online MIDI Sequencer, (requires a web browser and QuickTime Player plugin installed)

PianoRollComposer - Windows

Sekaiju - Windows

Loop-based MIDI sequencers

harmonySEQ - Linux

Seq24 - Linux, Windows

Scorewriters

MuseScore - Linux, Windows, Mac

DAW with MIDI sequencers

Frinika - Java (cross-platform)

LMMS - GNU/Linux, Windows

MusE - Linux

Qtractor - Linux

Rosegarden - Linux

Loop-based audio sequencers

ThunderBeatD3 - Windows XP Vista 7 (freeware)

Integrated software studio environments

The Buzz Machines - Windows

Drum machines

Hydrogen (cross platform, drum machine) - Linux, Mac OS X (Windows version discontinued)

Not categorized yet

Multitrack hard disk recorders

Ardour - Linux, Mac OS X, FreeBSD *(Note: No sequence feature found)*

Others

Commercial

MIDI sequencers

Numerology Modular step sequencer for Mac OS X

Bars and Pipes Professional - Amiga (classic) (gratis)

DAWs with MIDI sequencers

Ableton Live from Ableton Audio

Evolution from eXtream

Master Tracks Pro from GVOX
Improvisor, midi sequencer for generative music by Percussa, works together with AudioCubes

Realtime arrangers with MIDI sequencers
One Man Band

Piano training software
PianoCheetah - Windows (gratis) (*Guitar Hero* style)

Scorewriters
Musette - Windows (gratis)

Loop-oriented DAWs with MIDI sequencers
ACID Pro and Cinescore from Sony Creative Software
Live from Ableton
GarageBand from Apple
MU.LAB UL / XT / FREE - Windows
Software Development Cubase and Nuendo from Steinberg
Digital Performer from MOTU
energyXT from XT software
FL Studio from Image Line Software
Logic Pro and Logic Express from Apple
Metro from Sagan Technology
Mixcraft from Acoustica
Orion Platinum from Synapse Audio
Pro Tools from Avid
Samplitude, Sequoia, Mac OS (gratis)
REAPER from Cockos
Tracktion from Mackie

Tracker-oriented DAWs with MIDI sequencers
Renoise

Music Maker and Music Studio from Magix
SAWStudio with Midi Workshop from RML Labs
Sonar and Home Studio from Cakewalk
Studio One from PreSonus
Turbo Play (in test stage)
Usine from Sensomusic
Podium from Zynewave (gratis)
Z-Maestro from Z-Systems

Loop-based audio sequencers
Live Touch XJ, from Ematrade - Android 3.0 Honeycomb tablet
Loopseque from Casual Underground Lab - iPad/ iPhone

Integrated software studio environments
Reason and Record from Propellerhead
Project5 from Cakewalk
Storm from Arturia

Not categorized yet
Realtime orchestral accompaniments
Sinfonia, from Realtime Music Solutions *(Note: It seems not the sequencer)*
Hard Disk recorder solutions for MIDI sequencers
WinAudio from Zadok Audio & Media Products
Others
Source http://en.wikipedia.org/wiki/Music_sequencer

Variable-gain amplifier

A **variable-gain** or **voltage-controlled amplifier** is an electronic amplifier that varies its gain depending on a control voltage (often abbreviated CV).

VCAs have many applications, including audio level compression, synthesizers and amplitude modulation.

A crude example is a typical inverting op-amp configuration with a light-dependent resistor (LDR) in the feedback loop. The gain of the amplifier then depends on the light falling on the LDR, which can be provided by an LED (an optocoupler). The gain of the amplifier is then controllable by the current through the LED. This is similar to the circuits used in optical audio compressors.

A voltage-controlled amplifier can be realised by first creating a voltage-controlled resistor (VCR), which is used to set the amplifier gain. The VCR is one of the numerous interesting circuit elements that can be produced by using a JFET (junction field-effect transistor) with simple biasing. VCRs manufactured in this way can be obtained as discrete devices, e.g. VCR2N.

Another type of circuit uses operational transconductance amplifiers.

In audio applications logarithmic gain control is used to emulate how the ear hears loudness. David E. Blackmer's dbx 202 VCA was among the first successful implementations of a logarithmic VCA.

In sound mixing consoles

Some mixing consoles come equipped with VCAs in each channel for console automation. The fader, which traditionally controls the audio signal directly, becomes a DC control voltage for the VCA. The maximum voltage available to a fader can be controlled by one or more master faders called **VCA groups**. The VCA master fader then controls the overall level of all of the channels assigned to it. Typically VCA groups are used to control various parts of the mix; vocals, guitars, drums or percussion. The VCA master fader allows a portion of a mix to be raised or lowered without affecting the blend of the instruments in that part of the mix.

A benefit of VCA sub-group is that since it is directly affecting the gain level of each channel, changes to a VCA sub-group level affect not only the channel level, but also all of the levels sent to any post fader mixes. With traditional audio sub-groups, the sub-group master fader only affects the level going into the main mix and does not affect the level going to the post fader mixes. Consider the case of an instrument feeding a sub-group and a post fader mix. If you completely lower the sub-group master fader, you would no longer hear the instrument itself, but you would still hear it as part of the post fader mix, perhaps a reverb or chorus effect.

VCA mixers are known to last longer than non- VCA mixers. Because the VCA controls the audio level instead of the physical fader, decay of the fader mechanism over time does not cause a degradation in audio quality.

Digital variable-gain amplifier

A **digitally-controlled amplifier** (DCA) is a variable-gain amplifier that is digitally controlled.

The digitally controlled amplifier uses a stepped approach giving the circuit graduated increments of gain selection. This can be done in several fashions, but certain elements remain in any design.

At its most basic form, a toggle switch strapped across the feedback resistor can provide a two discrete gain settings. While this is not a computer controlled function, it describes the core function. With eights switches and eight resistors in the feedback loop, each switch can enable a particular resistor to control the feedback of the amplifier. If each switch was converted to a relay, a microcontroller could be used to activate the relays to attain the desired amount of gain.

Relays can be replaced with Field Effect Transistors of an appropriate type to reduce the mechanical nature of the design. Other devices such as the CD4053 bi-directional CMOS integrated circuit can serve well as the switching function.

To minimize the quantity of switches and resistors, combinations of resistance values can be utilized by activating multiple switches.

Source http://en.wikipedia.org/wiki/Variable-gain_amplifier

Voltage-controlled filter

A **voltage-controlled filter (VCF)** is a processor, a filter whose operating characteristics (primarily cutoff frequency) can be controlled by means of a control voltage applied to control inputs. It can be considered to be a frequency-dependent amplifier. Although popularly known for their use in analog music synthesizers, in general, they have other applications in military and industrial electronics.

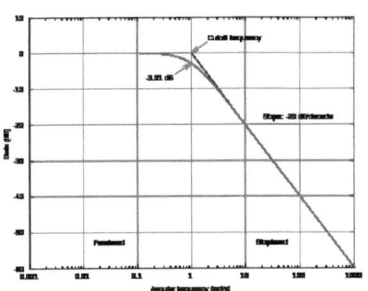

Depiction of cutoff frequency of a low-pass filter, showing Butterworth response

A VCF allows its cutoff frequency and Q (resonance at the cutoff frequency), Q factor, to be continuously varied; the signal outputs may include a low-pass response, a highpass response, a bandpass response, and a notch response. The filter may offer a variable *slope* which determines the rate of attenuation outside the bandpass, often at 6dB/octave, 12dB/octave (a '2 pole' filter) or 24dB/octave (a '4 pole' filter). This is also varied by the Q.

In modular analog synthesizers, filters receive signal input from signal sources (including oscillators oscillator(s)), and noise), or the output of other processors. By varying the cutoff frequency, the instrument passes or attenuates partials.

In some popular electronic music styles, "filter sweeps" have become a common effect. These sweeps are created by varying the cutoff frequency of the VCF (sometimes very slowly). Controlling the cutoff by means of a transient voltage control, such as an envelope generator, especially with relatively fast attack settings, may simulate the attack transients of natural or acoustic instruments.

Historically, VCFs have included variable feedback which creates a response peak (Q) at the cutoff frequency. This peak can be quite prominent, and when the filter's frequency is swept by a control, partials present in the input signal resonate. Some filters are designed to provide enough feedback to go into oscillation, and it can serve as a sine-wave source.

ARP Instruments made a multifunction voltage-controlled filter module capable of stable operation at a Q greater than 100; it could be shock-excited to ring like a vibraphone bar. Q was voltage-controllable, in part by a panel-mounted control. Its internal circuit was a classic analog computer state variable "loop", which provided outputs in quadrature.

A VCF is an example of an active non-linear filter: however, if its control voltage is kept constant, it will behave as a linear filter.

Source http://en.wikipedia.org/wiki/Voltage-controlled_filter

Voltage-controlled oscillator

A **voltage-controlled oscillator** or **VCO** is an electronic oscillator whose oscillation frequency is controlled by a voltage input. The applied input voltage determines the instantaneous oscillation frequency. Consequently, modulating signals applied to control input may cause frequency modulation (FM) or phase modulation (PM). A VCO may also be part of a phase-locked loop.

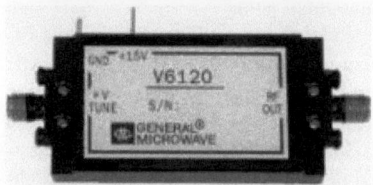

A microwave (12-18 GHz) Voltage Controlled Oscillator

Types of VCOs

VCOs can be generally categorized into two groups based on the type of waveform produced: 1) harmonic oscillators, and 2) relaxation oscillators.

Linear or **harmonic oscillators** generate a sinusoidal waveform. Harmonic oscillators in electronics usually consist of a resonator with an amplifier that replaces the resonator losses (to prevent the amplitude from decaying) and isolates the resonator from the output (so the load does not affect the resonator). Some examples of harmonic oscillators are LC-tank oscillators and crystal oscillators. In a voltage-controlled oscillator, a voltage input controls the resonant frequency. A varactor diode's capacitance is controlled by the voltage across the diode. Consequently, a varactor can be used to change the capacitance (and hence the frequency) of an LC tank. A varactor can also change ("pull") the resonant frequency of a crystal resonator.

Relaxation oscillators can generate a sawtooth or triangular waveform. They are commonly used in monolithic integrated circuits (ICs). They can provide a wide range of operational frequencies with a minimal number of external components. Relaxation oscillator VCOs can have three topologies: 1) grounded-capacitor VCOs, 2) emitter-coupled VCOs, and 3) delay-based ring VCOs. The first two of these types operate similarly. The amount of time in each state depends on the time for a current to charge or discharge a capacitor. The delay-based ring VCO operates somewhat differently however. For this type, the gain stages are connected in a ring. The output frequency is then a function of the delay in each of stages.

Harmonic oscillator VCOs have these advantages over relaxation oscillators.

Frequency stability with respect to temperature, noise, and power supply is much better for harmonic oscillator VCOs.

They have good accuracy for frequency control since the frequency is controlled by a crystal or tank circuit.

A disadvantage of harmonic oscillator VCOs is that they cannot be easily implemented in monolithic ICs. Relaxation oscillator VCOs are better suited for this technology. Relaxation VCOs are also tunable over a wider range of frequencies.

Control of frequency in VCOs

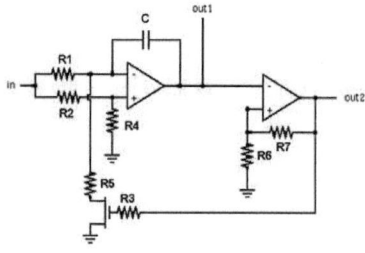

Voltage-controlled oscillator schematic - audio

A voltage-controlled capacitor is one method of making an LC oscillator vary its frequency in response to a control voltage. Any reverse-biased semiconductor diode displays a measure of voltage-dependent capacitance and can be used to change the frequency of an oscillator by varying a control voltage applied to the diode. Special-purpose variable capacitance varactor diodes are available with well-characterized wide-ranging values of capacitance. Such devices are very convenient in the manufacture of voltage-controlled oscillators For low-frequency VCOs, other methods of varying the frequency (such as altering the charging rate of a capacitor by means of a voltage controlled current source) are used. See Function generator.

The frequency of a ring oscillator is controlled by varying either the supply voltage, the current available to each inverter stage, or the capacitive loading on each stage.

Voltage-controlled crystal oscillators

A *voltage-controlled crystal oscillator* (*VCXO*) is used for fine adjustment of the operating frequency. The frequency of a voltage-controlled crystal oscillator can be varied a few tens of parts per million (ppm), because the high Q factor of the crystals allows "pulling" over only a small range of frequencies.

There are two reasons for using a VCXO:

To adjust the output frequency to match (or perhaps be some exact multiple of) an accurate external reference.

Where the oscillator drives equipment that may generate radio-frequency interference, adding a varying voltage to its control input can disperse the interference spectrum to make it less objectionable. See spread-spectrum clock generation.

A 26 MHz TCVCXO.

A *temperature-compensated VCXO* (TCVCXO) incorporates components that partially correct the dependence on temperature of the resonant frequency of the crystal. A smaller range of voltage control then suffices to stabilize the oscillator frequency in applications where temperature varies, such as heat buildup inside a transmitter.

Placing the oscillator in a temperature-controlled "oven" at a constant but higher-than-ambient temperature is another way to stabilize oscillator frequency. High stability crystal oscillator references often place the crystal in an oven and use a voltage input for fine control. The temperature is selected to be the *turnover temperature*: the temperature where small changes do not affect the resonance. The control voltage can be used to occasionally adjust the reference frequency to a NIST source. Sophisticated designs may also adjust the control voltage over time to compensate for crystal aging.

VCO time-domain equations

$$f_{tuning}(t) = K_o \cdot v_{in}(t)$$

$$\int f_{tuning}(t)\,dt = \theta_{out}(t)$$

K_o is called the oscillator gain. Its units are hertz per volt.

$f_{tuning}(t)$ is the symbol for the time-domain waveform that is the VCO's tunable frequency component.

$\theta_{out}(t)$ is the symbol for the time-domain waveform that is the VCO's output phase.

$v_{in}(t)$ is the time-domain symbol of the control (input) voltage of the VCO; it is sometimes also represented as $v_{tune}(t)$

VCO freq-domain equations

$$F_{tuning}(s) = K_o \cdot V_{in}(s)$$

$$\frac{F_{tuning}(s)}{s} = \Theta_{out}(s)$$

Analog applications such as frequency modulation and frequency-shift keying often need to control an oscillator frequency with an input — a voltage-controlled oscillator (VCO). The functional relationship between the control voltage and the output frequency may not be linear. Over small ranges, the relationship is approximately linear, and linear control theory can be used.

There are devices called voltage-to-frequency converters (VFC). These devices are often designed to be very linear over a wide range of input voltages.

VCO design and circuits

Tuning range, tuning gain and phase noise are the important characteristics of a VCO. Generally low phase noise is preferred in the VCO. The noise present in the control signal and the tuning gain affect the phase noise; high noise or high tuning gain imply more phase noise. Other important elements that determine the phase noise are the transistor's flicker noise ($1/f$ noise), the output power level, and the loaded Q of the resonator. See Leeson's equation. The low frequency flicker noise affects the phase noise because the flicker noise is heterodyned to the oscillator output frequency due to the active devices non-linear transfer function. The effect of flicker noise can be reduced with negative feedback that linearizes the transfer function (for example, emitter degeneration).

Leeson's expression for single-sideband (SSB) phase noise in dBc/Hz (decibels relative to output level per Hertz) is

$$L(f_m) = 10\log\left[\frac{1}{2}\left(\left(\frac{f_0}{2Q_l f_m}\right)^2 + 1\right)\left(\frac{f_c}{f_m} + 1\right)\left(\frac{FkT}{P_s}\right)\right]$$

where f is the output frequency, Q is the loaded Q, f is the offset from the output frequency (Hz), f is the $1/f$ corner frequency, F is the noise factor of the amplifier, k is Boltzmann's constant, T is absolute temperature in Kelvins, and P is the oscillator output power.

Commonly used VCO circuits are the Clapp and Colpitts oscillators. The more widely used oscillator of the two is Colpitts and these oscillators are very similar in configuration.

VCOs generally have the lowest Q-factor of the used oscillators, and so suffer more jitter than the other types. The jitter can be made low enough for many applications (such as driving an ASIC), in which case VCOs enjoy the advantages of having no off-chip components (expensive) or on-chip inductors (low yields on generic CMOS processes). These oscillators also have larger tuning ranges than the other kinds, which improves yield and is sometimes a feature of the end product (for instance, the dot clock on a graphics card which drives a wide range of monitors).

Applications

VCOs are used in:
Function generators,
The production of electronic music, to generate variable tones,
Phase-locked loops,
Frequency synthesizers used in communication equipment.
Voltage-to-Frequency converters are voltage-controlled oscillators, with a highly linear relation between applied voltage and frequency. They are used to convert a slow analog signal (such as from a temperature transducer) to a digital signal for transmission over a long distance, since the frequency will not drift or be affected by noise. VCOs may have sine and/or square wave outputs. Function generators are low-frequency oscillators which feature multiple waveforms, typically sine, square, and triangle waves. Monolithic function generators are voltage-controlled. Analog phase-locked loops typically contain VCOs. High-frequency VCOs are usually used in phase-locked loops for radio receivers. Phase noise is the most important specification for them. Low-frequency VCOs are used in analog music synthesizers. For these, sweep range, linearity, and distortion are often most important specs. Audio-frequency VCOs for use in musical contexts have largely been superseded by their digital counterparts, DCOs, due to their output stability in the face of temperature changes during operation.

Voltage-controlled crystal oscillator as a clock generator

A clock generator is an oscillator that provides a timing signal to synchronize operations in digital circuits. VCXO clock generators are used in many areas such as digital TV, modems, transmitters and computers. Design parameters for a VCXO clock generator are tuning voltage range, center frequency, frequency tuning range and the timing jitter of the output signal. Jitter is a form of phase noise that must be minimised in applications such as radio receivers, transmitters and measuring equipment.

The tuning range of a VCXO is typically a few parts per million over a control voltage range of typically 0 to 3 volts. When a wider selection of clock frequencies is needed the VCXO output can be passed through digital divider circuits to obtain lower frequency(ies) or be fed to a PLL (Phase Locked Loop). ICs containing both a VCXO (for external crystal) and a PLL are available. A typical application is to provide clock frequencies in a range from 12 kHz to 96 kHz to an audio digital to analog converter.

Source http://en.wikipedia.org/wiki/Voltage-controlled_oscillator